GREAT INVENTIONS

THE TELEGRAPH AND TELEPHONE

By Richard Worth

WORLD ALMANAC® LIBRARY

Please visit our web site at: www.worldalmanaclibrary.com
For a free color catalog describing World Almanac® Library's list of high-quality books and multimedia programs, call 1-800-848-2928 (USA) or 1-800-387-3178 (Canada). World Almanac® Library's fax: (414) 332-3567.

Library of Congress Cataloging-in-Publication Data

Worth, Richard.
     The telegraph and telephone / by Richard Worth.
        p. cm. — (Great inventions)
     Includes bibliographical references and index.
     ISBN 0-8368-5879-4 (lib. bdg.)
     1. Telephone—History—Juvenile literature. 2. Telegraph—History—Juvenile literature. I. Title. II. Great inventions (Milwaukee, Wis.)
     TK6165.W67   2005
     621.385'09—dc22   2005040777

First published in 2006 by
World Almanac® Library
A Member of the WRC Media Family of Companies
330 West Olive Street, Suite 100
Milwaukee, WI 53212 USA

Copyright © 2006 by World Almanac® Library.

A Creative Media Applications, Inc. Production
Design and Production: Alan Barnett, Inc.
Editors: Matt Levine, Susan Madoff
Copy Editor: Laurie Lieb
Proofreader: Tania Bissell
Indexer: Nara Wood
World Almanac® Library editor: Carol Ryback
World Almanac® Library art direction: Tammy West
World Almanac® Library production: Jessica Morris

Photo credits: Clip Art: pages 4, 10, 14, 19, 20, 22, 23, 28; © Bettmann/CORBIS: pages 5, 7, 16, 25, 33, 34, 38; © CORBIS: pages 13, 29; Associated Press Worldwide: pages 15, 39, 40; © Minnesota Historical Society/CORBIS: page 31; Photo.com: page 37; diagrams by Rolin Graphics.

Printed in Canada

1 2 3 4 5 6 7 8 9 09 08 07 06 05

TABLE OF CONTENTS

CHAPTER 1 Before the Telegraph and the Telephone.... 4

CHAPTER 2 Morse Invents the Telegraph............ 9

CHAPTER 3 Impact of the Telegraph 16

CHAPTER 4 The Invention of the Telephone........ 22

CHAPTER 5 Telephone Use Increases............... 28

CHAPTER 6 Communication in the
Twentieth Century.................... 33

CHAPTER 7 The Future 38

Time Line 44

Glossary 45

For More Information.................. 46

Index........................... 47

Words that appear in the glossary are printed in
boldface type the first time they appear in the text.

CHAPTER

1 BEFORE THE TELEGRAPH AND THE TELEPHONE

▼ *Carrier pigeons were used well into the nineteenth century to carry messages between troops during times of war. In 1870, during the siege of Paris, France, more than four hundred carrier pigeons aided the French troops.*

Imagine living in a time when the only way to communicate with another person was by face-to-face contact or by written word. People could not stay in their houses and talk to someone next door, across town, or in another state. News about things that happened in other places could take days or weeks to arrive. Communicating with someone elsewhere in the world took even longer: months or—sometimes—years.

The invention of the **telegraph** and the **telephone** made fast, reliable communication possible at any distance. These inventions meant that everyone could communicate instantaneously. As soon as someone had an idea, he or she could tell another person, even if that person were miles away. The invention of the telegraph and, later, the telephone led to the modern world of instant communications.

The World before the Telegraph and Telephone

In the ancient world, the Romans built a vast network of roads to link their far-flung empire. If the Roman emperor wanted to send a message, he dispatched a messenger. It took the messenger many days or weeks to arrive at the destination. Indeed,

4

some messengers never arrived at all because hostile troops intercepted them along the way.

During the thirteenth century, Genghis Khan tried to speed up communications. Khan and his Mongolian horsemen had conquered a huge empire in Asia and Europe. To make communications across the empire faster, Genghis Khan used carrier pigeons. He ordered his soldiers to set up relay stations across Asia. Carrier pigeons flew from station to station, carrying short messages attached to their bodies.

In North America during the fourteenth and fifteenth centuries, Native Americans built signal stations on high mounds to communicate with each other. Lookout scouts lit fires at their stations to signal others in villages many miles away. Historians believe that a fire signaled that an Indian village was under attack and needed help.

During the fifteenth century, the Inca, a South American civilization, controlled a vast empire. It stretched for more than 1,500 miles (2,400 kilometers) along the west coast of the South American continent, from present-day Peru north to what is now Colombia. A system of roads connected the empire. Since they had no horses, the Inca relied on runners to carry messages. Post houses built along the roads allowed a messenger to rest after running long distances. Another messenger stationed at the post house would then take the message and complete the next leg of the journey. In this way, messages traveled hundreds of miles in a few days.

In the eighteenth century, another form of long-distance communication was used in France. Towers were built from the Normandy Coast in the northwest to the capital at Paris, about 100 miles (160 kilometers) away. On top of each tower stood a tall wooden pole

▲ Native Americans used smoke from fires set atop high mounds to indicate success or failure in battle and to alert neighboring settlements of danger.

with a movable, horizontal bar of wood at the top. Flags attached to the ends of the wooden bar could be moved up and down to different positions. Each position indicated a letter. By changing the flags' positions, operators spelled out words and sent messages from tower to tower. Messages traveled from the Normandy Coast to Paris in the relatively fast time of four minutes.

Looking for Improvements

For centuries, these early methods of long-distance communication were the best options. They had serious drawbacks, however. Many methods were slow, while others worked only for short messages or needed daylight to be effective. People needed a method of communication that was faster and could carry more information.

In the middle of the eighteenth century, inventors in Europe and America started experimenting with a new science—electricity. At first, these inventions seemed completely unconnected to communications. Soon, however, scientists changed their way of thinking about electricity. During the eighteenth and early nineteenth centuries, inventors such as Benjamin Franklin, William Sturgeon, and Joseph Henry performed experiments with electricity that laid the foundations for long-distance communication by telegraph and telephone.

Benjamin Franklin (1706–1790) thought that electric current was a steady stream that could travel through metal, and he set out to prove it. In 1752, Franklin flew a kite during a severe thunderstorm. When the kite was struck by a lightning bolt, a piece of metal at the top of the kite conducted electricity from the lightning through the kite, down a silk thread, to a metal key. Based on what he learned from this experiment, Franklin invented the lightning rod. A lightning rod placed on a house conducts electricity through a wire to the ground, preventing the house from catching fire if it is hit by lightning. Franklin realized that electricity traveled quickly through a wire. He made no connection, however, between electricity and communication.

Meanwhile, scientists in Europe conducted other experiments with electricity. In 1753, Charles Marshall, a Scottish scientist, wrote, "It is well known to all who [understand] electrical experiments that electric power may be [sent] along a small wire from one place to another, without being sensibly [weakened] by the length of its progress." Marshall suggested stringing a series of wires from one point to another. Metal balls would be placed at the far end of each wire, and below each ball would lie a piece of paper with a letter of the alphabet on it. According to Marshall, electricity sent through one of the wires would produce a charge in the ball and attract a letter. In this way, words could be spelled out. Marshall, however, never experimented with his ideas; they were only theories.

Marshall's idea involved electricity as well as **electromagnetism**. The term *electromagnetism* means producing a magnetic charge in a piece of metal using electricity. Marshall had made an early connection between communication, electromagnetism, and electricity.

In 1800, Alessandro Volta (1745–1827), an Italian scientist, developed a simple battery using small disks of copper and zinc. He placed cardboard in between the disks and then soaked the device in saltwater. When he connected the disks with wire, an electrical charge ran

▼ *Alessandro Volta's research into electricity helped make the telegraph possible. Years later, Volta's simple battery was eventually improved upon to operate revolutionary communication devices.*

The power of the electric charge is called a volt, named after Alessandro Volta. Volta's inspiration for his battery, called the voltaic pile, occurred as he was observing the dissection of a frog whose legs began to twitch. After trial and error, Volta realized that the two metal objects holding the frog were the source of an electric current.

between them, from the negatively to the positively charged disk. Early batteries produced one or two **volts** of electric power. Volta's battery was a method of producing electricity that would later be used in communication devices.

Like Volta, other nineteenth-century scientists believed there was a connection between electricity and **magnetism**. In England in 1825, William Sturgeon (1783–1850) invented the **electromagnet**. Sturgeon took a piece of iron and wrapped wire around it. Electricity sent through the wire magnetized the piece of iron. The iron magnet attracted a 9-pound (4-kilogram) piece of metal and raised it off the ground. Over the next few years, Sturgeon built a more powerful electromagnet and became a popular lecturer on electricity.

In the United States during the 1830s, Joseph Henry (1797–1878) conducted important experiments involving electromagnetism. Henry taught math and physics at Albany Academy, a prep school for boys in Albany, New York. He read about the electromagnets developed by Sturgeon. Henry began building electromagnets and demonstrating them to his students.

In 1832, Henry hooked up a battery to a long piece of wire and ran it around a large classroom. At the other end of the wire was an electromagnet. He placed a steel rod and bell near the magnet. When Henry sent electricity through the wire to the magnet, it attracted the rod and rang the bell.

Henry thus demonstrated that electricity produced by a battery could be carried through a wire to an electromagnet and ring a bell. Sounding the bell was a simple type of communication, still used today in the common doorbell. The next step was to invent a way of using electric current to carry messages through wires over long distances.

2
MORSE INVENTS THE TELEGRAPH

T he verb *telegraph* means to write or send writing over a distance. Originally, it meant any kind of long-distance communication that used signals. During the nineteenth century, however, the word *telegraph* came to mean long-distance electronic communication.

Several components make up a telegraph. The sending unit consists of a moving lever called a code key that, when pushed down, completes an electric current. The coded series of electrical impulses travel by wire to the receiver, which translates the impulses into a printout. An electromagnet at the receiving end makes this possible by using electricity to create a magnetic field that, in turn, operates the printout mechanism.

◄ **A Simple Telegraph**
Depression of the code key completes an electric circuit and sends electric impulse through the wire. At the other end, an electromagnet, which consists of copper wire wound around a piece of iron, magnetizes the iron and causes it to "pull," or magnetically attract, a smaller metallic part and make a clicking sound. Every click or combination of clicks stands for a letter, and a series of letters spells out a word.

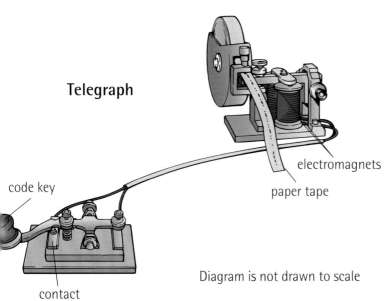

Telegraph

electromagnets

code key

paper tape

Diagram is not drawn to scale

contact

The Early Life of Samuel Morse

The man who finally put all of these elements together into a working telegraph was not trained as a scientist. He was a painter named Samuel F. B. Morse (1791–1872). Morse grew up in Charlestown, Massachusetts. While a student at Yale College in New Haven, Connecticut, he attended lectures on electricity and became interested in the possibilities it presented.

In 1829, Morse traveled to Europe to paint in France and Italy. On his return voyage to the United States, in 1832, aboard the sailing ship *Sully*, Morse met Dr. Charles T. Jackson (1805–1880). Jackson had read widely about electricity, and he spoke with Morse about the latest developments in the field. Together they discussed the possibility of creating an electric telegraph. Morse became very excited about transmitting electricity through a wire to produce long-distance messages. Morse even drew a picture of how the telegraph might work.

In November, the *Sully* docked at New York Harbor. As he was leaving the ship, Morse told the captain, "Well,...should you hear of the telegraph one of these days, as the wonder of the world, remember the discovery was made on board the good ship *Sully*."

▼ *Early telegraphs were mounted on wood to create a sturdy base for tapping out electrical signals.*

Morse Creates the Telegraph

In 1835, Morse became an art teacher at New York University in New York City. His students sometimes visited his living quarters. There, they watched

The Telegraph and Telephone

Morse experiment with an early telegraph and the batteries that produced electricity to run it.

Morse's telegraph was not the only telegraph **prototype** in the works. Charles Wheatstone (1802–1875), a British inventor and scientist, was working on a telegraph in England. Wheatstone used a series of wires attached to electromagnets. Electricity sent through a wire to an electromagnet activated a metal needle. The needle pointed to a letter on a chart that corresponded to the letter transmitted by the sender. In 1837, Wheatstone used his new telegraph to send a message more than 1.5 miles (2.4 km).

Wheatstone's invention was a complicated device. It included six wires and at least five metal needles. Working independently, Morse would soon create something much simpler that would revolutionize long-distance communication.

Samuel Morse was not an expert in electricity. He therefore had trouble figuring out how to send a message using electricity through a long wire. Morse received help from a colleague at New York University. Chemistry professor Leonard D. Gale realized that Morse needed a stronger battery to send electric current over long distances. Gale developed a thirty-nine-volt battery, replacing the one-volt battery that Morse had used earlier. Gale also recognized that Morse needed to increase the power of the electromagnet. Gale accomplished this by increasing the number of times the wire was wrapped around the magnet. With these improvements, Morse could operate the telegraph over a longer stretch of wire.

In September 1837, Morse demonstrated his telegraph at New York University. He succeeded in sending a message more than one-third of a mile. The wire through which the message was sent stretched around a lecture room at the university. One of Morse's former students, Alfred Vail, was present at the demonstration. Vail was so impressed with the telegraph that he volunteered to become Morse's assistant.

Morse also worked on a relay system to increase the distance over which a message could be sent. As the electric message reached an electromagnet at the end of a long stretch of wire, the magnet had just enough power to operate another **electric circuit**. Once this circuit was completed, the electronic message continued along another stretch of wire to the next **relay station**. As a result of Morse's invention, messages could now be sent over much longer distances. Even so, Morse had not constructed a practical telegraph. Before he got to this stage, Morse decided to conduct several demonstrations.

Morse Code

To send messages, Morse originally created a code using numbers. A series of dots and dashes indicated a number, such as 325. Each number equaled a word. A telegraph operator received the number and then looked in a special dictionary to find the word represented by the number. This system was very slow, so Morse and Vail worked out a letter code. Called the Morse code, it became the standard code used by telegraph operators in 1844.

The original Morse code, known as American Morse Code, was revised by German Friedrich Gerke in 1848. Known as the International Morse Code, it became the standard used throughout the world by 1865 and remains so today. The International Morse Code is a simplified form of the original version and differs in 11 letters, all the numerals (except the numeral 4), and the punctuation code.

International Morse Code

A · –	B – · · ·	C – · – ·	D – · ·	E ·	F · · – ·	G – – ·
H · · · ·	I · ·	J · – – –	K – · –	L · – · ·	M – –	N – ·
O – – –	P · – – ·	Q – – · –	R · – ·	S · · ·	T –	U · · –
V · · · –	W · – –	X – · · –	Y – · – –	Z – – · ·		

Morse Demonstrates the Telegraph

Early in 1838, Morse began to demonstrate the telegraph. At the Speedwell Iron Works, he sent a message along 2 miles (3.2 km) of wire to Vail's father. He strung the wire around a large room, just as he had at New York University, but this time the wire was much longer. The message stated, "A patient waiter is no loser."

In February 1838, Morse demonstrated the telegraph in front of President Martin Van Buren. In 1842, New York congressman Charles Ferris submitted a request to Congress for funding for the telegraph. He had seen Morse demonstrate the device and believed in its potential. Congress approved the idea and in March 1843 gave Morse $30,000 for the telegraph project.

Lightning Man

Morse immediately got to work, supervising the laying of telegraph wire from Washington, D.C., to Baltimore, Maryland, about 44 miles (71 km). He hired workers to dig long trenches in which to bury the wire underground. Morse then decided to put the wire inside lead tubes to protect it. Unfortunately, the tubes were not made properly and damaged the wire. Morse decided to stop the work of laying the cable underground. In March 1844, his crews began stringing the forty-four miles of wire on high wooden poles.

Finally, Morse was ready to test the new line. A political convention was being held in Baltimore to nominate a candidate for president. Long before the information could be carried from Baltimore to Washington, D.C., by train, Vail transmitted it by telegraph: Senator Henry Clay of Kentucky was nominated for president.

ALFRED VAIL, 1844

Alfred Vail

Alfred Vail (1807–1859) was thirty when he saw the first demonstration of the telegraph. Vail lived at the same small hotel in New York City as Morse did. Vail's father was a wealthy merchant who owned the Speedwell Iron Works in Morristown, New Jersey. From the training he received at the iron mill, Alfred Vail learned how to build mechanical devices. His knowledge was invaluable in developing the telegraph. Vail convinced his father to invest in the telegraph. Vail also persuaded his father to allow Morse to use the ironworks to develop new electronic devices. In 1837, Vail and Morse formed a partnership to work on the telegraph.

▲ *Tape from a telegraph machine consisted of a series of dots and dashes that was translated by operators into words. Some operators could tap out more than forty words per minute.*

On May 24, 1844, Morse demonstrated the telegraph line in Washington, D.C., once again. One end of the line was in Baltimore. Morse set up the other end of the line in the Supreme Court chambers in Washington, D.C. Morse's friend, Anne Ellsworth, was at his side and composed the first message. It was a quote from the Bible: "What hath God wrought!" Morse tapped out the message with his telegraph key to Baltimore.

In late 1844, Morse used the telegraph to transmit the results of the presidential election to Washington, D.C. In the election, Henry Clay had been defeated by James K. Polk.

News of the telegraph began to spread. People throughout America began referring to the new device as the "Lightning Line" because it could carry messages so quickly. Morse became known as "Lightning Man."

Expanding the Telegraph Lines

Morse received additional funds from Congress to run the Baltimore–Washington, D.C., line. He wanted, however, to expand the system to other cities. In this effort, he received the help of Amos Kendall (1789–1869). Kendall was a highly influential politician in Washington. Kendall began finding investors to finance telegraph lines to other cities. In 1845, he set up the Magnetic Telegraph Company—America's first telegraph company. The new company began expanding the telegraph line to Philadelphia,

Pennsylvania. Kendall formed another company that expanded the line to New York State. In 1846, telegraph lines connected New York City and Boston, Massachusetts. Other lines ran between Troy, in New York State, and Montreal, Canada.

Over the next ten years, telegraph lines stretching approximately 42,000 miles (67,200 km) were hung from poles spread across many parts of the United States. These lines linked together states on the Atlantic seaboard with territories in the West.

Business owners used the telegraph lines to confirm that shipments of goods reached their destinations. Newspaper reporters also relied on the telegraph to send news stories to their home offices. In 1846, the U.S. went to war with Mexico. Once the news from the battlefield arrived in Washington, D.C., it was immediately telegraphed to New York City and printed in the pages of the *New York Herald*.

The early telegraphs used printers to record the dots and dashes. But before long, experienced operators were using **sounders**. The sounder included an electromagnet. Electricity carrying a message from a sending station ran through a wire to the sounder. This turned the sounder into an electromagnet, attracting a piece of metal, which resulted in loud clicks when the metal and sounder made contact. The clicks created a series of dots and dashes that spelled out the letters and words that had been transmitted by the sender. Some operators could send and receive more than one hundred letters per minute.

Morse's long struggle had been richly rewarded. His telegraph brought him great financial success, and he retired to a large estate on the Hudson River in New York.

Fast Fact

Telegraph operators had to know the language of the telegraph well, and some highly skilled operators learned to recognize words by the telegraph's clicks. Ms. Abbie Strubel, who studied telegraphy at a school set up by the Baltimore & Ohio Railroad in Pittsburgh, Pennsylvania, in the 1860s, found her skills in demand when she became one of the earliest operators to "receive" messages by sound alone.

▼ The receiving end of the first telegraph typed out the message "What Hath God Wrought!" on May 24, 1844.

3 IMPACT OF THE TELEGRAPH

The telegraph changed the way people across America communicated. Soon telegraph wires stretched over the North American continent, and in 1866, a telegraph cable was laid along the floor of the Atlantic Ocean to connect the United States and Europe.

Western Union Strings the First Transcontinental Telegraph

▼ The Western Union Telegraph office in 1881 was a hive of activity. The noise of hundreds of operators tapping out messages on the telegraphs was almost deafening.

In 1851, a team of investors led by business executive Hiram Sibley (1807–1888), formed the New York and Mississippi Valley Printing Telegraph Company. Gradually, the company expanded, putting up lines westward from New York. In 1856, Sibley consolidated his company with others and renamed it Western Union Telegraph.

Sinking the Poles

Holes for the transcontinental telegraph had to be dug 5 feet (1.5 meters) into the ground to sink the poles. The telegraph workers had to span 1,100 miles (1,760 km). The workers had to battle heat, lack of water, and buffalo. The enormous beasts scratched their backs against the telegraph poles, knocking them down. Telegraph crews had to replace many poles.

Under Sibley's leadership, work began in 1861 to create a single telegraph line across the United States. The first telegraph poles began to go up during the summer of 1861. The line was completed in four months, far less than the expected time of two years.

There were still problems with the telegraph that had to be worked out. A message could not be sent from one end of the continent to the other. A single telegraph station could not create a strong enough electrical signal to cover the whole distance. Instead, a message was sent to a relay station, where an operator received the message and tapped it out to the next station.

The new line immediately began making money, because telegraph service was expensive. Sending a ten-word telegram from San Francisco, California, to St. Louis, Missouri, cost the high price of five dollars. An additional dollar was added to reach New York City or Washington, D.C. Five or six dollars was about one week's pay for many people.

The Telegraph and the Civil War

In 1861, the first message sent over the new transcontinental telegraph line from California was, "May the Union Be Perpetuated." While the telegraph line was being constructed across the West, rumblings of a civil war were beginning in the eastern part of the United States. Southern states had begun leaving the Union in 1860, following the election of Abraham Lincoln as president. They formed a new government, called the Confederate States of America. War between the Confederate and Union armies broke out in 1861. A year later, the Confederacy introduced the first ironclad ship, the *Merrimac*. A Union telegraph operator, George Cowlam, watching the *Merrimac* in Hampton Roads, Virginia, sent out the first reports as the iron-clad ship attacked Union ships on the coast. One of its victims was the *Cumberland*. "The *Merrimac* is steer-ing straight for the *Cumberland*," Cowlam tapped out over the telegraph. "She has rammed the *Cumberland* . . . the *Cumberland* is sinking, she has fired her last broadside [series of shots] and gone down."

During the war (1861–1865), covered wagons with telegraph equipment and wires accompanied the armies. In 1864, General Ulysses Grant led the Union army southward through Virginia to Richmond, the capital of the Confederacy. Telegraph operators put up poles and strung wire as the army advanced. The oper-ators often risked their lives as they became the targets of Confederate sharpshooters. These telegraph lines enabled Grant to coordinate the movement of his vast

Western Union

Western Union immediately put a competing company out of business. The Pony Express was a post system that had been founded in April 1860. Riders on horseback carried messages 10 to 12 miles (16 to 19 km) between relay stations. At each station, a rider handed the message to another rider who took it to the next station. The Pony Express carried messages about 2,000 miles (3,200 km), from St. Joseph, Missouri, to Sacramento, California, in ten days. The new telegraph carried the messages over that same distance almost instantaneously. The Pony Express went out of business after eighteen months in October 1861.

army, more than one hundred thousand men, as it moved southward.

In 1865, the Civil War ended at Appomattox, Virginia, with the surrender of Confederate general Robert E. Lee. Grant immediately telegraphed to President Lincoln in Washington, D.C.: "General Lee surrendered the army of Northern Virginia this afternoon on terms proposed by myself."

▲ *This picture from the late 1800s shows two telegraph poles put up in the middle of someone's farm. Telegraph poles became a familiar sight in the early twentieth century when they sprang up in rural areas across the United States.*

Laying the Transoceanic Cable

Perhaps the greatest challenge for telegraph communication was connecting North America with Europe. Making this connection was the dream of a successful and very rich business executive, Cyrus Field (1819–1892). Field was fascinated by the telegraph. In 1857, he hired men to begin working on the first stage of the transatlantic cable. The cable was flexible metal tubing housing the telegraph wires inside. A telegraph line first had to be stretched across Newfoundland and connections made to New York City. When this line was complete, Field was ready to lay the cable from Ireland to Newfoundland. This was a distance of about 2,000 miles (3,200 km). Two ships, the *Agamemnon* and the *Niagara*, were assigned to lay the heavy cable across the Atlantic. In August, the ships left Ireland.

The work went smoothly until the ships passed the 200-mile (320-km) point from land. The cable had to be laid carefully, with just the right speed and tension. A strong brake on the cable coil was designed to keep it under control. Early one morning, as the cable was being laid, the brake bore down too tightly on the cable, snapping it. The cable came loose and could not be recovered from the bottom of the Atlantic Ocean.

Fast Fact

Samuel Morse was an investor in Field's cable company. By the late 1860s, Morse was a very rich man. In 1871, a statue of Morse was unveiled in Central Park in New York City. When Morse died the following year, he was called the "first inventor of his age and century."

Impact of the Telegraph

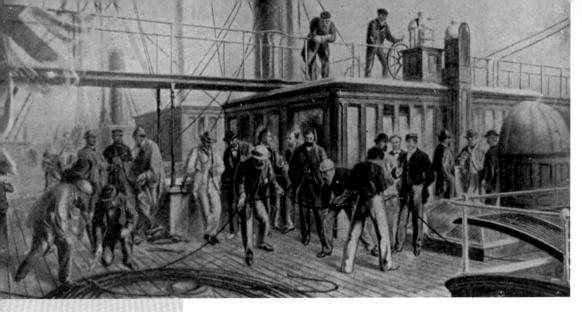

Field did not give up. In 1858, he tried again. This time the *Niagara* and the *Agamemnon* succeeded in completing the cable. A message was sent from Queen Victoria of England to President James Buchanan in the United States. After twenty-eight days of service and more than seven hundred messages, however, the cable broke. Scientists at the time were not sure why it failed.

In 1865, the British ship *Great Eastern,* 700 feet (210 m) long, began laying cable across the Atlantic. Because of its size, the ship could carry 2,000 miles (3,200 km) of cable—the entire distance from Ireland to Newfoundland. During the *Great Eastern*'s first attempt, the cable broke. But the following year, the *Great Eastern* was successful.

Advances in the Telegraph

During the 1870s, improvements to the telegraph continued. New wires were developed that allowed operators to send two messages at the same time. More cables were laid across the Atlantic Ocean, so a larger number of messages could be sent between the United States and Europe. More and more people

The Telegraph and Telephone

also used the telegraph in America. In New York City alone, the number of messages handled by Western Union zoomed from 3,500 in 1871 to ten times that number four years later.

Becoming a telegraph operator seemed like a promising career for many young people. They had to master the Morse code and then learn how to send messages as quickly as possible. Some of the operators worked in tiny offices in small towns. Others transmitted messages out of large Western Union offices, where the click of many telegraphs was almost deafening. Good operators could send and receive at about forty words per minute.

A few operators worked for the Associated Press (AP). This was a group of newspapers that worked together to find stories and report them. In 1875, the AP established its own telegraph lines to transmit stories from its reporters. Other operators worked for the railroads, helping to coordinate train traffic along tracks that crisscrossed America. The telegraph was also used by police departments. Police stations were connected by a telegraph wire. A telegraph operator in one police station could transmit information about a crime to another station.

In a few years, however, the telegraph would be overtaken by another invention—the telephone. The telephone would carry the human voice instead of dots and dashes. As a result, the need for the telegraph waned.

Telegraph Operator Contests

In the 1870s and 1880s, telegraph operators competed in contests. Several top operators would be given messages to transmit. The two operators who sent their messages with the fewest errors were given prizes. In one contest, the winning operator transmitted messages for five minutes at over fifty words per minute with only a single mistake.

During the nineteenth century, the United States was in the midst of the Industrial Revolution. New devices were continually being invented that changed transportation, communication, and the way people worked. New inventions sometimes made old ones obsolete—that is, no longer so useful. Perhaps the best example is the telephone, which gradually took the place of the telegraph in general use.

Early Life of Alexander Bell

The word *telephone* means to speak at a distance. The inventor of the telephone was a Scot named Alexander Graham Bell (1847–1922). Born in Edinburgh, Scotland, Alexander Bell was the son of Melville Bell, a world-famous elocutionist. Elocution is the art of public speaking. Melville Bell studied and wrote many prominent books on speech and language.

In 1860, Bell's father took him to meet the scientist and inventor Sir Charles Wheatstone. Years earlier, Wheatstone had invented a form of telegraph. He had also developed a machine that

▼ *Alexander Graham Bell's first telephone was a primitive machine. Sounds caused the light-colored disk (a soft leather membrane) to vibrate and transmit the sounds through the wires.*

could speak. "I saw Sir Charles manipulate the machine and heard it speak," Bell wrote, "and although the [speech] was disappointingly crude, it made a great impression on my mind."

Alexander and one of his brothers decided to build a speaking machine. They created a model of a human skull out of hard rubber. They also built a tongue, lips, and a larynx—the human voice box. When they pumped air into the machine, it made a sound like a baby crying "Mama." Creating the model was difficult. "Many times were we discouraged and disheartened over our efforts and ready to give the whole thing up in disgust," Bell later admitted. But they kept on working and learned an important lesson: Don't give up.

▲ Alexander Graham Bell demonstrates the telephone to a group of investors and scientists at the Centennial Exhibition in Philadelphia, Pennsylvania in 1876.

The Development of an Inventor

Bell admired his father's work and began to follow in his footsteps. In 1861, he began teaching elocution in Scotland. Bell began making experiments with human speech. He noticed that vowel sounds could be reproduced by using tuning forks. A tuning fork, a device that has a pitch that never changes, is used by musicians to tune their instruments.

In 1871, Bell moved to the United States and assumed teaching positions at different schools for deaf children. He used his father's visible speech program to teach the children how to speak. Bell had also learned that all sounds, including the sound of the human voice, make vibrations. He instructed the children to place balloons next to their chests. Bell reasoned that the children would feel the sounds of nearby wagons and horses on the street as the vibrations from these sounds struck the balloons.

Visible Speech

When Alexander Bell was a child, his father was working on a book titled *A Class-Primer of English Visible Speech.* Melville Bell had developed a way to depict each sound in speech as a symbol or picture showing the position of a person's lips and tongue when they produced that sound. This idea opened up an amazing new world for people who were deaf. Bell realized that human beings learn to speak by hearing the sounds of speech. Since people who were deaf could not hear these sounds, they could not reproduce them. By imitating the picture symbols, however, people who were deaf could learn to make the proper sounds.

Meanwhile, Bell was reading about efforts to improve the telegraph. Inventors were experimenting with ways to send not just one message, but multiple messages over a telegraph wire simultaneously. In 1872, Bell developed a telegraph that could send two messages by using different tones produced from two different tuning forks. As Bell sounded each tuning fork, the sounds went through separate wires to electromagnets at the other end. The magnets attracted two tuning forks, duplicating the original sounds.

Bell's work with the telegraph took him in a new direction. In 1873, he had become a professor at Boston University, where he tinkered with all types of electronic equipment. In 1874, he put together a device called a **phonautograph**. Bell used a complete human ear, which had been taken from a dead body. Attached to the inner ear was a reed. (A reed is a thin strip of material that vibrates to produce a tone when a stream of air passes over it.) As Bell spoke into a speaker attached to the ear, the bones in the inner ear vibrated and moved the reed. The movement of air over the reed resulted in sounds bouncing off a piece of glass. Bell wondered whether the same method might be used to set up electrical waves.

Sound vibrations hitting a thin membrane, like the membrane in the ear, might create electrical waves. These could travel through an electrical wire, striking a membrane at the other end, which would reproduce them as sound.

The Race to Be First

Bell's experiments interested Gardiner Hubbard, the rich father of one of his deaf students. Hubbard was fascinated with the possibilities of the phonoautograph. Bell and Gardiner Hubbard formed a partnership in 1874, with Hubbard financing the research.

While Bell was working on a telephone, other inventors were working on the same device. One of them was Elisha Gray (1835–1901). Gray had already received a patent for a telegraph relay. Gray was also working on a telegraph that could send eight messages at the same time, using eight tuning forks. "It is a neck-and-neck race between Mr. Gray and myself who shall complete our apparatus first," wrote Bell to his parents late in 1874.

Bell, however, was far more interested in developing a device to transmit the human voice rather than multiple messages using dots and dashes. Bell was not sure, however, that he understood electricity well enough to develop a new speaking device. Bell decided to get some advice from one of America's foremost scientists, Joseph Henry.

▼ Although inventor Elisha Gray did not get credit for the invention of the telephone, his work at Western Electric aided in the improvement and sophistication of telephones and other communication devices to come.

At their meeting, Bell explained his idea to transmit human speech. Henry called it "the germ of a great invention" and told Bell to keep working on it.

Bell Invents the Telephone

To help him with the mechanics of building his invention, Bell worked with a machinist named Thomas A. Watson. On June 2, 1875, Bell and Watson were experimenting with the multiple telegraph. In one room, Watson plucked one of the tuning forks that made a tone. The vibrating fork set up a current that flowed through a wire into another room where Bell was working. The current created an identical sound on the fork in Bell's receiver.

Bell believed that he was on the trail of developing a working telephone that could reproduce sound. He and Watson continued to experiment with a speaking device. On July 1, 1875, they tested another machine. Bell spoke into a membrane, vibrating a steel reed that set up a current in an electromagnet. The current flowed along a wire to a similar device. Watson could almost make out some of Bell's words.

Gardiner Hubbard, in an effort to protect his business interests and investment in Bell, instructed his lawyers to file a patent for the telephone. Although Bell was not yet ready for a patent, Hubbard's lawyers submitted the application on February 14, 1876. At almost the same time, Elisha Gray applied for a "patent caveat" at the U.S. Patent Office. The caveat was a notice that Gray was also working on "a speaking telephone." Gray's application reached the patent office a few hours after Bell's. As a result, Bell was granted U.S. Patent No. 174,465 on March 7, 1876. This meant that he was given credit for the invention of the telephone and the money it might make in the future.

The Telegraph and Telephone

Create Your Own Telephone

The principles of the early telephone can be re-created with two cleaned, rinsed, and dried food cans and a piece of string. Remove the lid from one end of each can. Cut a tiny hole in the other end, and connect the two cans with the string. Tie a knot at each end of the string, so it doesn't slip through the holes in the cans. Holding one can, walk away from your partner, who holds the other can, until the string is tight. As your partner talks into the open end of the can, put your can up to your ear and listen. Speak in a normal tone, and the words will be easy to hear.

Sound creates vibrations against the solid end of the can. This acts as a membrane, causing vibrations to move along the string. When the vibrations reach the other can, they produce sound.

The first telephone developed by Bell included a speaking tube with a membrane made of soft leather attached to one end. From the membrane, a needle was suspended into a small cup of water and acid. An electric wire ran from the acid to a similar device, which acted as a receiver. On March 10, 1876, Bell and Watson were working on this device. Bell was in his workshop with his speaking tube, while Watson was standing in another room with the duplicate device. Suddenly, Watson heard Bell say, "Mr. Watson, come here, I want you." The words were clear and understandable. Watson answered, "Mr. Bell, do you understand what I say?"

Each man's words, in turn, had vibrated the membrane, causing the needle to move up and down in the mixture of water and acid. This set up a vibration in the mixture that mimicked the vibration of speech. The vibration was reproduced as an electric current and carried across the wire to the receiver, which vibrated another membrane that produced speech. The telephone had been born.

5 TELEPHONE USE INCREASES

During the 1870s, Alexander Graham Bell continued to improve the telephone. He helped found the Bell Telephone Company, which pioneered long-distance and transcontinental telephone service.

The Centennial Exhibition

▼ *Telephone operators manage a switchboard in the late 1800s.*

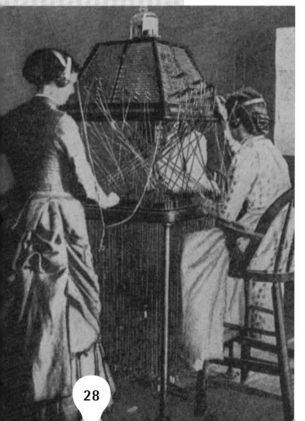

Philadelphia, Pennsylvania, hosted the 1876 International Centennial Exhibition. This world's fair celebrated the hundredth anniversary of the Declaration of Independence. New inventions, such as giant steam engines that powered large locomotives, were on display at the exhibition. With Gardiner Hubbard's encouragement, Bell arranged to demonstrate his new telephone at the fair.

On Sunday, June 25, the day Bell was scheduled to demonstrate the telephone, he spotted an old friend in the audience. Dom Pedro II (1825–1891), the emperor of Brazil, had met Bell earlier in the spring at the Boston School for the Deaf in Massachusetts. Bell showed Dom Pedro the telephone. Bell went into one room to speak into a transmitter, while Emperor Dom

Pedro remained in the room with the receiver. Meanwhile, the emperor was joined by the judges who were evaluating the inventions on display at the exhibition. Suddenly Bell spoke some words from a Shakespearean play. In the other room, the emperor cried out, "I have heard! I have heard!"

It was just the type of publicity that Bell needed. One of the judges, a famous physicist, declared: "I was astonished and delighted; so were the others, including some judges of our group who witnessed the experiments and verified with their own ears the electric transmission of speech."

▲ This early twentieth-century photograph shows storefronts and an intersection in Shreveport, Louisiana. Telephone poles run the length of the street, indicating that many storeowners were using the telephone to conduct business.

Early Breakthroughs

Later that year, Bell and Watson had a telephone conversation using two miles of telegraph wire already strung from Boston to the nearby town of Cambridgeport. These early telephones had a transmitter for speaking and a separate receiver for listening. By August 1877, there were already almost eight hundred telephones in operation. Gardiner Hubbard leased the telephones to people who wanted them. Charles Williams, an associate of Bell's, installed the first residential telephone line. It connected Williams's home with the workshop where he made telephone equipment. In 1877, Hubbard, Watson, and Bell started the Bell Telephone Company. The company charged residential customers $20 per year and business customers $40 per year. This was considered a fairly high price for the time period.

In 1878, the Bell Company introduced the Butterstamp telephone. It hung on a wall. Attached to the unit was a handheld receiver/transmitter. A person spoke into one end, then turned it around and listened at the other end. At first, many people were not sure they wanted or needed a telephone. The telegraph seemed sufficient to transmit messages rapidly. Bell Telephone, in its advertisements, reminded Americans that using the phone was much easier than the telegraph, since they did not need to learn Morse code.

The number of telephone users began to grow. Soon it became too expensive and too impractical to string separate wires between each set of callers who wanted to talk to each other. As a result, the telephone **switchboard** developed. A person who wanted to make a call would ring up a local switchboard, also known as an **exchange**. A bell rang in the exchange, alerting an operator that a call was coming through. The operator spoke to the caller, found out the person to whom the caller wished to speak, and then flipped a switch to con-

Switchboard Operators

The first switchboard operators were boys who were often rude to customers. Beginning in September 1878, when Emma and Stella Nutt were hired in Boston as the first female operators, young, single women began replacing boys on the switchboards. They were far more courteous. Gradually, female operators were hired for switchboards across the country. These women played an important role in the lives of many families. If someone contacted the switchboard and couldn't complete a call, the operator would take a message and deliver it when the other party had returned home. Operators knew callers by name and chatted with them while connecting the call. This kind of friendly relationship between operators and phone customers continued until the 1920s, when electronic switchboards began replacing operators.

nect the call to that person's line. The first switchboard was placed in service in New Haven, Connecticut, in 1878.

Battling Western Union

The Bell Telephone Company was facing stiff competition from a communications giant, Western Union. The company had a huge advantage over Bell because it owned telegraph lines across the United States and the early telephones used telegraph lines to make connections. Western Union also used a telephone apparatus developed by Elisha Gray. The company claimed that Gray, not Bell, had actually developed the telephone. In 1878, Bell Telephone sued Western Union for patent infringement. Alexander Bell himself testified in court. His testimony was so strong that Western Union lost the case and was forced out of the telephone business.

Wiring the Nation with Telephone Lines

During the 1880s, a forest of telephone poles sprang up in major cities across the United States. In New York City, telephone lines connected homeowners and businesses, enabling people within the City to speak with each other almost instantaneously. Long-distance lines also ran between cities in separate states, connecting Boston and New York City, and Washington, D.C. with Boston. Copper wire replaced iron wires, enabling the human voice to travel farther. Sometimes callers encountered problems as they tried to speak with each other. Calls were mysteriously interrupted by conversations from other telephone lines. Electrical storms created heavy static along the lines. The intro-

wire

▲ *A climber adjusts wire on a utility pole in rural Minnesota in the early twentieth century. Many Irish immigrants arriving in the United States during this time found work putting up poles and stringing wire across the country.*

The Cost of Phone Service

Telephone service was not cheap. During the 1880s, a homeowner was asked to pay $70 per year for service. The first five hundred calls were free, and then a caller had to pay six cents per call. This rate reached $100 by the 1890s—far beyond the means of many Americans. Innovative telephone executives developed cheaper alternatives. Among these was the party line. A group of ten people living in an apartment house shared the same telephone line. Another alternative was pay telephones. Callers could go to a telephone booth and complete a call for five cents. The first pay telephone was installed in Hartford, Connecticut, in 1889.

duction of electric lights on city streets and electric subways added to the interference. Improvements, such as insulating the wires, gradually eliminated the interference. Telephone companies also began to lay wires underground.

During the first decade of the twentieth century, there were already more than six million telephones in service in a nation of about ninety million people. Some of the lines provided local service, others long-distance service. The most successful provider of long-distance service was American Telephone and Telegraph Company (AT&T). In 1899, AT&T and Bell were joined together in the same company, which was known as AT&T during the twentieth century. During much of the century, AT&T had a complete monopoly on long-distance service. Anyone who wanted to make a telephone call across the country had to use the AT&T long-distance lines. In 1974, however, the federal government required competition in the long-distance market. By the mid-1980s, companies such as Sprint began to compete with AT&T.

The telephone was changing the United States and the world. No communications device as efficient and useful as the telephone had ever existed before.

The Telegraph and Telephone

COMMUNICATION IN THE TWENTIETH CENTURY

During the early twentieth century, AT&T hooked up millions of homes and businesses with local and long-distance telephone service. Meanwhile, new inventions made the telephone even more powerful. Calls could be completed across the United States and from North America to Europe.

Growth of Telephone Use

Under the direction of Theodore Vail, AT&T bought up smaller telephone companies. Vail invested heavily in research, developing devices that would boost the sound of the human voice so that calls could be made over longer and longer distances. Much of the research was conducted at the Western Electric Company, founded by Elisha Gray. Started in 1869, Western Electric made equipment for inventors. Later the company was bought by Bell, and it continued manufacturing equipment for AT&T.

The scientists at AT&T were unable to invent a device that would provide enough power to carry the human voice across the North American

▼ *Theodore N. Vail, president of the Bell and American Telephone Company, was responsible for bringing the telephone into the modern age by investing in research that focused on the range and quality of calling.*

▲ *Inventor Lee De Forest holds up his audio tube invention, which improved the sound quality of long-distance calls.*

continent. Inventor Lee de Forest (1873–1961) solved this problem. As a young inventor, de Forest built telegraph stations that communicated with each other using radio waves instead of wires. In 1907, de Forest received a patent for the Audion. This was a **vacuum tube**. It consisted of a glass container with little or no air inside, two pieces of metal, and a metal grid in between them. The Audion picked up radio signals, and the metal grid boosted the signal.

De Forest demonstrated the Audion to Western Electric in 1911. Led by Harold Arnold, the Western Electric engineers improved the vacuum inside the glass tube. This enabled sounds picked up by the tubes to be boosted, or amplified, even louder. Meanwhile, Theodore Vail publicly announced that transcontinental telephone service would be available by 1914. The new vacuum tubes, invented by de Forest and perfected by AT&T engineers, could make coast-to-coast service possible.

Under the leadership of John Carty, chief engineer of AT&T, more than 300 miles (482 km) of line were built from Denver, Colorado, westward to Salt Lake City, Utah. From San Francisco, California, wire was strung 700 miles (1,120 km) eastward to Utah. On June 17, 1914, the line was completed. Now 130,000 telephone poles connected the United States from coast to coast.

On January 25, 1915, Alexander Graham Bell and Thomas Watson spoke on a coast-to-coast hookup. Bell was stationed in New York City, and Watson was in San Francisco. "Hoy, hoy, Mr. Watson, are you there? Do you hear me?" Bell said.

"Yes, Mr. Bell, I hear you perfectly. Do you hear me well?" Watson said.

"Yes, your voice is perfectly distinct," Bell replied.

New Uses for the Telephone

About five weeks after the transcontinental telephone line was completed, World War I (1914–1918) broke out. The United States entered the war in 1917. To assist the U.S. army, telephone workers enlisted in the service. They joined the Signal Corps and served in France. They strung 100,000 miles (160,000 km) of wire and set up one hundred switchboards. More than two hundred U.S. female telephone operators managed switchboards for the U.S. army in Europe. The phone systems helped the Allied commanders direct their troops and defeat the German army.

By the 1920s, the telephone had become a familiar part of American life. New telephone desk sets—with the transmitter and receiver combined into a single handheld unit that looked much like many telephones today—were introduced, and telephone service started to become automated. During the 1930s, telephone lines were increasingly laid underground to reduce the number of overhead wires. In addition, improved wiring systems led to better telephone service.

During the 1930s, dial telephones were introduced. The dial sat atop the main portion of the telephone, which had the numbers one through nine and a zero printed on it in a circle counterclockwise from right to left. Each dial had ten finger holes around its outside edge, with one number visible through each hole. A caller put a finger in a hole—the hole over number six, for example—and rotated the dial clockwise to a preset stopping point. Removing the finger from the

Theodore Vail

Theodore Vail (1845–1920) was a cousin of Alfred Vail, who had worked with Samuel Morse on developing the telegraph. Theodore Vail worked as a telegraph operator for Western Union in Rochester, New York. During the 1860s, he met Gardiner Hubbard, who persuaded him to come to work for the Bell Telephone Company in 1878. During the 1880s, as general manager of Bell Telephone, Vail helped expand the company's telephone business into small towns throughout the country. His attitude was, "Let's take a chance. That area needs telephones as much as any other." Vail had a vision of bringing telephone service to homes and communities throughout the United States. Later, as president of AT&T, Vail spent millions of dollars on research and pioneered the development of transcontinental service. Vail retired as president of AT&T in 1919 and died a year later.

Telegraph and Telephone

Telephones became increasingly popular in the early twentieth century. By 1900, there were already one million phones in the United States. The telegraph, however, did not completely disappear. In fact, in 1929 alone, 200 million telegrams were sent in the United States. Many people did not own a telephone, and the telegraph was still considered a very reliable form of long-distance communication—even more dependable than the telephone. Accounts of major league baseball games were telegraphed to radio stations as the games were being played and broadcast by announcers. Singing telegrams were also popular: Messengers sang greetings from well-wishers to someone celebrating a birthday. During World War II (1939–1945), Western Union messengers brought government telegrams announcing the deaths of soldiers killed in combat to homes across the United States.

hole allowed the dial to rotate back to its original position, thus sending out six electric pulses.

Each telephone number consisted of a sequence that sent out a series of pulses that were routed through automatic switching machines. These first appeared during the 1920s. They enabled many calls to be automatically connected without operators. The use of dial phones and automatic switching replaced many switchboards and operators during the 1920s and 1930s.

Telephone Innovations

As automatic switching machines replaced operators, telephone companies introduced the dial tone. This was an important new technology. In the past, a caller had picked up a telephone and asked for an operator. "Number, please," the operator said to the caller and connected the call. In the 1950s, the dial tone was gradually installed on many telephone lines. It told a caller that a line was available. Direct dialing enabled callers to make calls by themselves.

Telephones also became more stylish. In the late 1950s and throughout the 1960s, many of the black phones were gradually replaced by colored telephones—blue, pink, white. Then, in 1959, AT&T introduced a new, smaller phone with a lighted dial, called the Princess phone. These came in a variety of colors and were marketed to the increasing number of affluent U.S. families as a second phone. Trimline phones, introduced in 1965, had the dial on the inside of the receiver instead of on the base of the set.

During the early 1950s, AT&T perfected new technology for undersea telephone cables. In 1956, telephone cables connecting the United States with Europe were completed at a cost of $42 million. On the first day of telephone service, 588 calls were made across the Atlantic.

In 1963, the first touch-tone telephones were introduced. Instead of dials, they contained push buttons. By pushing a sequence of buttons, callers produced tones indicating the telephone number of the person they were trying to reach. The tones sent signals to computerized switching stations that routed the calls.

Telephones had come a long way since their invention by Alexander Graham Bell, but much more was still to follow.

▲ *Rotary, or dial, telephones were the first to come in a variety of colors. Additional styles through the years contributed to the increased numbers of phones people had in their homes. Rotary phones were eventually phased out when touch-tone telephones and service became available.*

Electronic Switching

One of the major breakthroughs during the middle of the twentieth century was electronic switching systems. These systems used computers to connect calls. AT&T scientists worked on these systems from the 1940s through the 1970s until they were serving millions of customers across America. Without electronic switching, the vast number of calls placed today could not be made.

7

THE FUTURE

O ver the past few decades, telephone communication has changed dramatically. Telephones have improved greatly as a result of recent electronic inventions, such as tiny **transistors**, large communication satellites, and vast radio-cell networks.

The Impact of the Transistor

The invention of transistors, which replaced vacuum tubes, revolutionized a wide array of electronic equipment. Made of silicon, which is found in sand, transistors contain several minute electronic circuits. One circuit takes in an electronic signal, another circuit increases the strength of the signal, and a third circuit passes on the signal to another location. Packed into televisions, radios, computers, and telephone equipment, transistors enable these products to shrink in size and, at the same time, become more powerful. The use of transistors to boost telephone signals began during the 1960s.

Transistors are used in digital telephones and digital switching stations. These stations receive calls by the thousands. A digital switch changes the electric signal

▼ *The transistor contains several minute electronic circuits, all designed to increase and transport a signal from one location to another. Their tiny size revolutionized many inventions, including the telephone. These three transistors sit on top of a dime. The three prongs on the transistor serve as terminals that control current or voltage.*

produced by the human voice on a telephone line into combinations of impulses. A coast-to-coast call may pass through several switching stations. At each one, the signal is boosted by transistors so that it can be heard on a telephone many miles away.

Communications Satellites

The introduction of satellites has also had an enormous impact on communications. In 1962, Telestar became the first communications satellite to be sent aloft into Earth's atmosphere. Today, more than 250 satellites orbit the globe and transmit television images, radio programs, and telephone communications.

Each satellite has a large receiving antenna, usually shaped like a large dish, to receive communications from Earth. The signals, called an uplink, travel long distances from the ground to the satellites. **Transponders** on the satellites receive the communications signals and boost their power. These signals, called a downlink, are then sent by the satellite's transmitter antenna to a receiving station back on Earth. Satellites enable telephone callers in North America to make rapid connections with people in Europe, South America, Australia, Africa, or Asia.

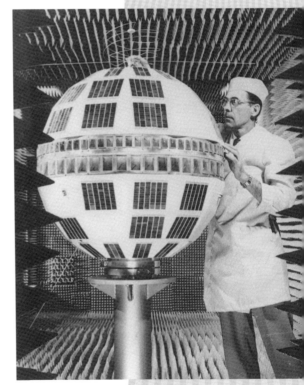

▼ This 1962 photograph shows engineer Charles A. Haas with a model of the Telestar communications satellite at the Bell Telephone Company laboratory in Hillside, New Jersey. Satellite technology continues to improve communication around the world today.

Cordless Phones

Today, many callers use wireless telephones to place their telephone calls. In the past, callers were forced to remain in one place and use a telephone connected by a short cord to an electrical outlet. Cordless telephones allow callers far greater mobility. With a cordless telephone, callers can walk around their home or office while talking. A cordless telephone changes the human voice into radio waves. These radio waves are transmitted from the antenna on the handset to the base of the telephone. From there, the signal is changed into electrical impulses and sent along the telephone system.

Cellular Telephones

Cellular telephones (cell phones) are another type of wireless communication that has transformed the industry. Cell phones are very small and completely portable. People walking down a street or standing outside a school building can talk to someone in another neighborhood, another town, or another country. They no longer need to find a phone or a phone booth because they carry the cell phone in their pocket or purse. Wherever people are, they can make or receive a call.

Dr. Martin Cooper is the inventor of the cell phone. Born in 1930, Cooper went to work for Motorola, a large electronics company, in 1954. He worked on a variety of portable telephones. These included mobile telephones that relied on radio waves. Mobile phones were used by police, who carried them in the police cars. To make calls, the police officer contacted a mobile telephone operator. The operator then sent the call along the telephone wires to the nearest radio receiving station. The station transmitted the call to another police car. By 1973, Cooper developed a successful cell telephone, the Motorola Dyna-Tac. It was large com-

▼ Dr. Martin Cooper first publicly demonstrated the cellular phone pictured below while walking down a street in New York City in April 1973. Since it was still years before the invention of a cordless telephone, onlookers stared at the sight of a man speaking into a phone that wasn't connected to wires of any kind. Cell phones would not become common until the early 1990s.

pared to today's cell phones—9 inches (22.8 centimeters) long and 5 inches (12.7 cm) wide. It weighed 2.5 pounds (1.2 kg). Cooper created a cell station in the state of New York. Then, on April 3, 1973, he walked along a street in New York City, talking on the phone. As Cooper recalled, "Sophisticated New Yorkers gaped at the sight of someone actually moving around while making a phone call."

It took another ten years to refine the working of the phone and sell it. Over the next two decades, cell phones were purchased by millions of people across the world.

The cell telephone takes its name from a geographical area called a cell. Each **cell station** includes a tower with antennas to receive **microwave radio signals** transmitting calls. As callers speak on their cell phones, the calls are sent to the cell tower by microwave radio signals and from there to a switching station. The station routes the call to another tower in a different cell where the call is completed. Cell systems use low-powered equipment within each cell. As a result, each cell can use the same channels as a nearby cell, without interfering with calls in any other cells. This enables millions of telephone customers to talk on the system at the same time.

The first cell phones, developed in the 1970s, were big, bulky, and expensive. Now cell phones are small, lightweight, and cheap. Cell phone use grew quickly around the world. During the 1980s, western European nations established the Global System for Mobile Communications. These nations worked together to build cells across Europe. Cell phones are also widely used in Asia, especially in Japan. Cell phones are so convenient that some people have removed traditional plug-in telephones from their homes.

Fast Fact

The first portable cell phone call was made by Dr. Martin Cooper, a general manager at Motorola and the inventor of the cellular phone. In April 1973, Dr. Cooper called Joel Engel, his rival and head of research at Bell Labs, to surprise him and prove that Cooper's system was operational!

Telephones, Pictures, and Data

Digital telephone communications translate not only the human voice into electronic impulses but other types of information, too. **Facsimile** (fax) machines became popular during the 1980s and 1990s. The fax machine includes an electronic scanner that picks up light waves from a picture or printed material. These light waves are changed into electric impulses representing the digits 0 and 1. The impulses are sent along a telephone system to a receiver. The telephone receiver converts them back into print or images and records them on paper. The fax machine enables users to send long reports over the telephone lines much more rapidly than by mail. Attorneys, for example, can send lengthy contracts to their clients immediately, so business can be conducted in a matter of hours instead of days.

Many telephones contain other communication devices. These include built-in answering machines. They record information from a caller when someone is unavailable to receive a call. An answering machine prevents people from missing important calls. Many calls do not require a two-way conversation. A caller may only want to transmit information, such as the message "I will be late for our lunch. Please wait for me at the restaurant." Therefore, an answering device can save valuable time. It does not provide, however, the same friendly service as the telephone operators in the past who took messages for callers.

Another feature, known as call-waiting, alerts someone who is on the telephone that another caller is trying to get through. The person can put the first call "on hold" and talk to the second caller. Call forwarding immediately transfers a call from one telephone number to another, which allows the user to answer the call in a more convenient location or even

The Telegraph and Telephone

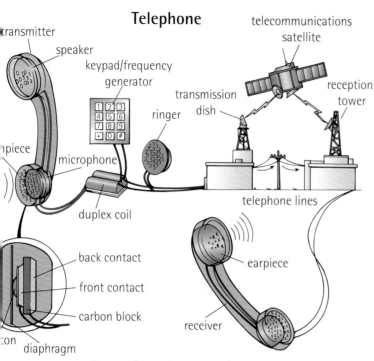

Telephone

transmitter
speaker
keypad/frequency generator
piece
microphone
ringer
transmission dish
telecommunications satellite
reception tower
telephone lines
duplex coil
back contact
front contact
carbon block
receiver
earpiece
con diaphragm

Diagram is not drawn to scale

while moving to another location. Many cell phones offer these features as well as visual messaging. For instance, a cell phone may contain a tiny camera that can take still photos or short videos and transmit them to another cell phone number or a computer. Also, some cell phones can send and receive e-mail, hook up to the Internet, and provide instant text-messaging. In fact, most cell phones today contain miniaturized computer technology that is more powerful than the computers that helped send astronauts to the Moon!

Communications Superhighway

Today, it's easy to take the communications super-highway for granted. A century ago, it did not exist. Samuel Morse's telegraph and Alexander Graham Bell's telephone helped create the communications network of the twenty-first century, bringing the world closer together into a single global community.

◀ To make a telephone call, the caller presses a series of numbered buttons on a keypad that match the number of the telephone he or she is trying to reach. Pressing these buttons sends electric impulses along the telephone network to a switching station. There, computers receive the impulses and route the call to the phone number the caller wants to contact. The impulses cause the receiving phone to ring. When the person answering the call picks up the phone, the connection is made, and the caller begins speaking. A device called a duplex coil blocks the sound of the caller's voice from coming through to the speaker and causing an echo.

Some conversations are transmitted only over land lines; that is, telephone wires. However, long-distance calls are often sent to transmitting stations and beamed via microwaves to a communication satellite. The satellite transmits calls to a reception tower that, in turn, sends them along land lines to the receiving numbers.

TIME LINE

1752	Benjamin Franklin conducts famous experiment with kite and electricity.
1753	Charles Marshall writes about early telegraph.
1800	Alessandro Volta demonstrates a way to produce electricity.
1825	William Sturgeon invents the electromagnet.
1844	Samuel F. B. Morse sends telegraph message from Washington, D.C. to Baltimore
1845	Magnetic Telegraph Company is founded.
1856	Western Union Telegraph is formed.
1861	The transcontinental telegraph line is completed. The telegraph is used to transmit messages during the Civil War. The Pony Express is put out of business by Western Union.
1865	The *Great Eastern* successfully lays the transatlantic telegraph cable, making telegraph service between North America and Europe possible.
1875	The Associated Press establishes its own telegraph lines.
1876	Alexander Graham Bell receives a patent for the telephone.
1877	The Bell Telephone Company is founded.
1878	The Butterstamp telephone is introduced.
1899	AT&T and Bell Telephone Company join together.
1907	Lee de Forest receives a patent for the Audion.
1915	Transcontinental telephone service becomes available.
1917–1918	Telephone workers assist American troops in World War I.
1930s	Dial telephones are introduced.
1940s	Western Union messengers deliver government telegrams announcing the deaths of soldiers in World War II to homes across the United States.
1950s	The dial tone is installed on telephone lines. The Princess phone is introduced.
1956	AT&T connects the United States and Europe with telephone cables.
1962	Telestar becomes the first communications satellite to be sent into Earth's atmosphere.
1963	Touch-tone telephones are introduced.
1973	The cell telephone is developed.
1980s	AT&T is ordered by the U.S. government to dismantle the company. Fax machines become standard items in offices and homes.
1990s	Internet use becomes available via telephone lines.
21st century	Cell telephones with cameras to record pictures and short videos are introduced.

GLOSSARY

cell station: location with antenna to receive cell calls

cellular telephones (cell phones): wireless phones that operate by radio waves

digital telephone communications: the transmission of digital information over telephone systems

electric circuit: an electrical device that provides a path for electrical current to flow

electromagnet: a piece of metal magnetized by the force of electricity

electromagnetism: magnetism produced by an electric charge in motion

exchange: telephone switchboard

facsimile: transmission of photographs and data by electric signal

magnetism: a force that enables pieces of metal to attract each other

microwave radio signals: a method of transmitting data using high-frequency radio waves. It requires a line of sight between sending and receiving stations

phonautograph: a forerunner of the telephone that sent sounds

prototype: an original, full-scale, and usually working model of a new product or new version of an existing product

relay station: an intermediate station that passes information between terminals or other stations; telegraph messages would travel long distances by being transmitted from one relay station to the next

sounders: the electromagnetic devices on telegraphs that, when in contact with metal, created loud clicks that translated into a series of dots and dashes to spell out letters and words

switchboard: an early device for connecting multiple telephone calls

telegraph: electronic device that sends coded messages long distance

telephone: electronic device that sends the human voice long distance

transistors: tiny devices that control electric current and boost sound

transponders: a radio or radar transmitter-receivers

vacuum tube: a device that amplifies sound

volts: units of electric power

FOR MORE INFORMATION

Books

Alter, Judy. *Samuel F. B. Morse: Inventor and Code Creator.* Minnesota: Child's World, 2003.

Dasanellas, Antonio. *Great Discoveries and Inventions that Advanced Industry and Technology.* Wisconsin: Gareth Stevens Publishing, 2000.

Gearhart, Sarah. *Turning Point Inventions: The Telephone.* New York: Atheneum, 1999.

Grosvenor, Edwin, and Morgan Wesson. *Alexander Graham Bell: The Life and Times of the Man Who Invented the Telephone.* New York: Harry N. Abrams, 1997.

McCormick, Anita Louise. *The Invention of the Telegraph and Telephone in American History.* New Jersey: Enslow Publishers, 2004.

Pasachoff, Naomi. *Alexander Graham Bell: Making Connections.* New York: Oxford University Press, 1996.

Videos and DVDs

Biography: Alexander Graham Bell: Voice of Invention. New York: A&E Home Video, 2003.

Modern Marvels: Great Inventions. New York: A&E Home Video, 2003.

The Story of Alexander Graham Bell (1939). New York: 20th Century Fox Home Entertainment, 1996.

Web Sites

www.acmi.net.au/AIC/TELEGRAPHY_LULA.html Story of the evolution of sound in communication with details of Samuel Morse's experiences with the telegraph.

www.inventors.about.com/library/inventors/bltelephone.htm Web site features a history of both Alexander Graham Bell's telephone and Elisha Gray's invention.

www.pbs.org/wgbh/amex/telephone/peopleevents/index.html Web site offers background information on the important contributors to the invention of the telegraph and telephone.

INDEX

Agamemnon (ship)
19, 20
American Civil War
17–19
American Telephone
and Telegraph
Company (AT&T)
success of 32
telephone innova-
tions 37
telephone service of
33–34
Theodore Vail
and 35
answering machine 42
Associated Press
(AP) 21
Atlantic Ocean
telephone cable
across 37
transoceanic
telegraph cable
19–20
Audion 34
automatic switching 36

battery 7–8, 11
Bell, Alexander Graham
at Centennial
Exhibition 28–29
communications
today and 43
development as
inventor 23–25
early life of 22–23
invention of tele-
phone 25–27
long-distance call
34–35
telephone break-
throughs 29–31
Bell, Melville 22,
23, 24
Bell Telephone
Company
founding of 28
satellite and 39
telephone break-
throughs 29–31
telephone use,
growth of 33–35
Theodore
Vail and 35

Buchanan, James 20
Butterstamp
telephone 30

cable
telegraph,
laying of 13
telephone 37
transcontinental tele-
graph cable 16–17
transoceanic tele-
graph cable 19–20
call forwarding 42–43
call-waiting 42
carrier pigeons 4, 5
Carty, John 34
cellular telephones
development of
40–41
features of 43
first commercial sys-
tem for 42
Clay, Henry 14
communication
experiments for
improvements
6–8
superhighway 43
telegraph, impact of
16–21
telegraph, invention
of 9–15
communications
satellite 39
Cooper, Martin 40–41
cordless phones 39–40
cost of
telegraph service 17
telephone service
29, 32

De Forest, Lee 34
dial telephones 35–37
dial tone 36–37
digital switching sta-
tions 38–39
digital telephone com-
munications 42–43
downlink 39

electricity
experiments with
6–8

idea for telegraph
and 10
invention of
telegraph and
11–12
in telegraph process
9–10
electromagnet
invention of 8
Morse's telegraph
11
in sounder 15
in telegraph
process 9
electromagnetism 7, 8
electronic switching
systems 37
Ellsworth, Anne 14
exchange 30–31

facsimile (fax)
machines 42
Federal
Communications
Commission (FCC) 42
Ferris, Charles 13
Field, Cyrus 19–20
Franklin, Benjamin 6–7

Gale, Leonard D. 11
Genghis Khan 5
Global System
for Mobile
Communications 41
Grant, Ulysses 18–19
Gray, Elisha 25, 26, 31
Great Eastern (ship) 20

Haas, Charles A. 39
Henry, Joseph 25–26
experiments of 6, 8
Hubbard, Gardiner
leased telephones 29
partnership with
Alexander Bell
25, 28
telephone
patent and 26
Theodore
Vail and 35

Industrial
Revolution 22

interference 31–32
International Centennial
Exhibition 28–29

Jackson, Charles T. 10

Kendall, Amos 14–15

Lafayette,
Marquis de 11
Lee, Robert E. 19
lightning 6–7
lightning rod 7
light waves 42
Lincoln, Abraham 18
long-distance calls
33–35
long-distance telephone
service 32

Magnetic Telegraph
Company 14–15
magnetism 8
Marconi, Guglielmo 21
Marshall, Charles 7
mobile telephones
features of 43
first commercial sys-
tem for 42
introduction of
40–41
Monroe, James 11
Morse code 12, 21, 30
Morse, Samuel F. B.
communications
today and 43
creation of telegraph
11–13
early life of 10
success of 19
telegraph demonstra-
tions by 13–14
telegraph lines 14–15
Motorola 40–41

Native Americans 5, 6
New York and
Mississippi Valley
Printing Telegraph
Company 16
Niagara (ship) 19, 20
Nutt, Emma
and Stella 30

pay telephone 32
phonautograph 24
pigeons, carrier 4, 5
poles, telegraph 17
Polk, James K. 14
Pony Express 18
Princess phone 37

radio waves 40, 41
Romans 4–5
rotary telephones
  35–37

satellite 39
Sibley, Hiram 16–17
Signal Corps 35
signals 39
silicon 38
singing telegrams 36
sounder 15
Speedwell Iron
  Works 13
Sturgeon, William 6, 8
Sully (sailing ship) 10
switchboard operators
  30, 35
switchboard, telephone
  development of
    30–31
  replacement of 36
switching, automatic 36
switching station,
  digital 38–39

tape 14
telegraph
  advances in 20–21
  Alessandro
    Volta and 7

Alexander Graham
  Bell and 24, 26
American Civil War
  and 17–19
components of 9–10
continued use of 36
defined 9
demonstrations of
  13–14
expansion of lines
  14–15
idea for 10
invention of 11–13
telephone competi-
  tion 31
transcontinental
  telegraph 16–17
transoceanic cable
  19–20
world before 4–6
telegraph lines
  expansion of 14–15
  laying of first 13–14
  transcontinental
    telegraph 16–17
telegraph operator 21
telephone
  Alexander Graham
    Bell and 22–25
  breakthroughs 29–31
  cellular telephones
    40–41
  cordless phones
    39–40
  innovations 36–37
  lines 31–32
  new uses for 35–36
  photograph
    of first 22

pictures/data with
  42–43
race to invent 25–27
satellite and 39
time line 44
transistor, impact of
  38–39
Western
  Union and 31
telephone lines
  improvements 35
  putting up 31–32
telephone operators
  28, 35, 36
telephone service
  29, 32
Telestar satellite 39
touch-tone
  telephones 37
transcontinental
  telegraph 16–17
transcontinental tele-
  phone service 33–35
transistor 38–39
transoceanic cable
  19–20
transponders 39
Trimline phones 37
tuning forks 23,
  24, 26

uplink 39

vacuum tube 34
Vail, Alfred 12, 13, 35
Vail, Theodore N.
  life of 35
  telephone use and
    33, 34

Van Buren, Martin 13
volt 8
Volta, Alessandro 7–8

Watson, Thomas A.
  invention of tele-
    phone and 26, 27
  long-distance call
    34–35
  telephone break-
    throughs 29
Western Electric
  Company 33, 34
Western Electric
  Manufacturing
  Company 26
Western Union
  Telegraph
  Bell Telephone
    Company and 31
  messages
    handled by 21
  Pony
    Express and 18
  telegrams delivered
    by 36
  transcontinental tele-
    graph 16–17
Wheatstone, Charles
  Alexander Graham
    Bell and 22–23
  telegraph invention
    by 11
Williams, Charles 29
wireless telephones
  39–41
wires, telephone 31–32
World War I 35
World War II 36

Author Biography

Richard Worth is the author of more than fifty nonfiction books for young adults. These include biographies, history, and current events, as well as a series on the criminal justice system. In 2004, his book, *Gangs and Crime*, was named one of the Best Books for the Teenage List by the New York Public Library. Worth also runs training programs in business writing and public speaking for Fortune 100 companies in the United States and Europe. In addition, he has been a volunteer teacher of writing to third graders in the Bridgeport, Connecticut, public school system for the past decade.